AF284291

# Taihu Lake Qigong

## Hartmut von Czapski

# Taihu Lake Qigong

## Hartmut von Czapski

**Imprint**

Bibliographic information from the German National Library:
The German National Library lists this publication in the German National
Bibliography; detailed bibliographical data can be found on the Internet at
http://dnb.dnb.de.
© 2020 Hartmut von Czapski
Photographs by Ellen and Hartmut von Czapski
Production and publishing: BoD - Books on Demand, Norderstedt
ISBN: 9783751916479

Table of Contents

# About the author

Hartmut von Czapski

Non-medical practitioner since 1984. Since 1987 exercise of acupuncture (Teacher Fr.Dr. Li Te, Chief Physician Nankei Clinic). Several stays in China with professional trainings.
1987 Scientific training of Uni.Tübingen passed: "Ecology and its biological basis".
Since1990 seminars, yoga and Qi Gong courses at various institutes. Since 1990 more than 1000 Qi Gong classes have been held.
Qi Gong Teacher 49009 des Mi Gong Rulai Buddhist Center for Qi Gong, Shanghai.
Training to Qi Gong Therapeut by Prof. Wu, Shanghai. Lectures at the Medica in Dusseldorf on the treatment of incontinence with T.C.M .
1999 acupuncture specialist training for dentists; Teacher activity on various therapies.

Teaching Qi Gong Forms:
Medical Qi Gong according to Prof.Wu.
Taiji Qigong after Li Ding.
Ten meditations on the mountain Wudang.

The Eighteenfold Method of Exercise.
The "Movements of the 5 Animals".
Qi Gong after Guo Lin for immune boosting.
The "Eight elegant exercises. "
"Wai dan gung"
"Tai Hu Lake Qi Gong"
Tai Chi for beginners by Dr. med. Jiang Hao-quan. And much more.

## Qi Gong

The term "Qi Gong" includes various types of exercises to absorb the "Qi", the life energy, and let it flow in the energy channels, the so-called "meridians". It is a substance that you normally do not see and grope, but can feel. The ancient Chinese philosophers thought that Qi is a source substance that originated in the Big Bang.

According to the Chinese view, Qi is a continuously moving and active substance, the basic substance from which the body originates. Qi receives the human life functions. By definition Qi in Qi Gong is an "essence" substance in the body with a certain energy. Qi can be formed, developed, transformed and moved in the body. Breathing moves the energy in the meridians. But even after a long practice of Qi Gong, one can move and absorb qi with the mind in the body.

These body and breathing exercises have at least a 4000-year-old tradition in China, as can be seen in descriptions of funerary offerings. There are many different types of exercises. On the one hand the soft Qi Gong, which contains many meditative elements based on the imagination and is often performed while sitting or lying down. On the other hand, we know the hard Qi Gong, which also strengthens the muscles and tendons and massages the internal organs.

Think e.g. to the achievements of the Shaolin monks in Kung Fu or to the acrobatic skills of the actors of Peking Opera. But Qigong exercises not only strengthen the body, but also calm the mind and regulate the autonomic nervous system.

A special form is the therapeutic qigong, which prescribes certain exercises for certain illnesses. Like any empirical science, qigong is always being developed. For example, in recent decades, e.g. certain new exercises against cancer are famous for their good results (Qi Gong after Guo Lin for improving the immune system). The high blood pressure research institute Shanghai has already published in 1978 works with reports on changes that causes Qigong on the ECG and EEG. Work has also been published that our sympathetic nervous system, which is active through prolonged stress, achieves relaxation through Qi Gong by predominance of the parasympathetic nervous system.

In China, in many hospitals, in addition to the Department of Medicine, there is a Department of Traditional Chinese Medicine. This includes the treatment room for the Qi Gong therapist. Here the patient is not only taught exercises that he should practice regularly at home, the therapist also supplies the patient with energy that he himself has absorbed.

Training to become a Qi Gong therapist is usually tedious. After 5 years of practice, you can teach Qi Gong exercises and also treat after 10 years. Mr. von Czapski has been trained by Prof.Wu as a Qi Gong therapist.

## Important energy centers
Hui Yen, KG1. In the middle of the perineum, between the anus and the sex.

"Real" Dantian. It lies between the navel and the spine. Lower Dantian, about 2 fingers wide under the navel. Approx. at the acupuncture point "Qi Hai", sea of energy.

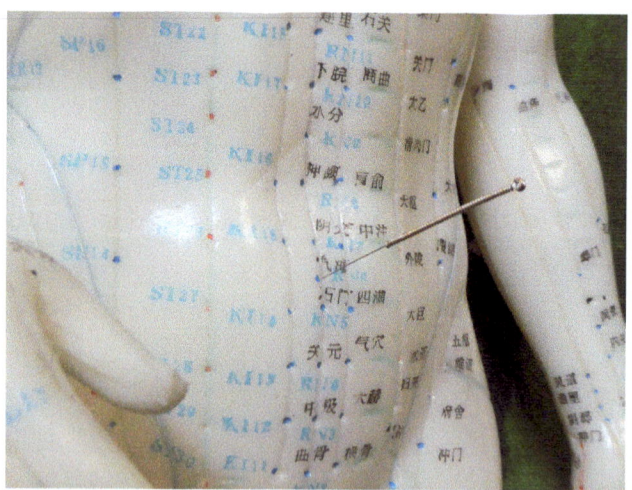

Middle Dantian, heart center. At the level of a hollow on the sternum, between the nipples. "Tan Zhong" (KG17).

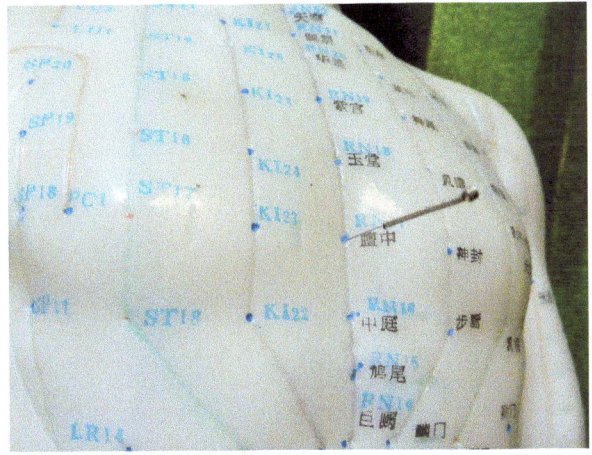

Upper Dantian, "Yintang". Between the eyebrows, just above the bridge of the nose.

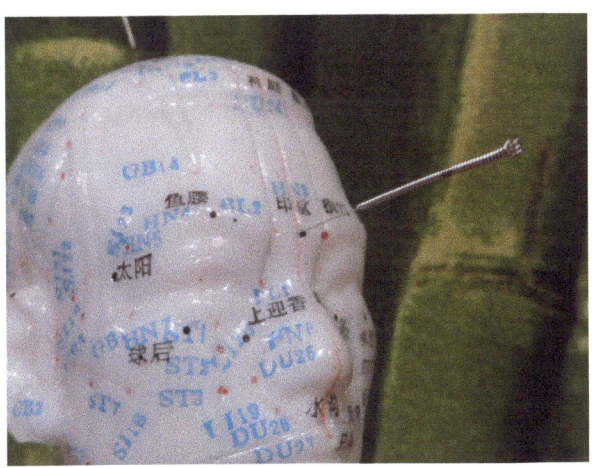

Bai Hui. Located in the middle of an imaginary line between the tips of the ears in a small hollow.

Mingmen. If you put the top of your index finger under the back of your costal arch and stretch your thumb towards your spine, you can use your thumb tips to reach the Mingmen point on the spine.

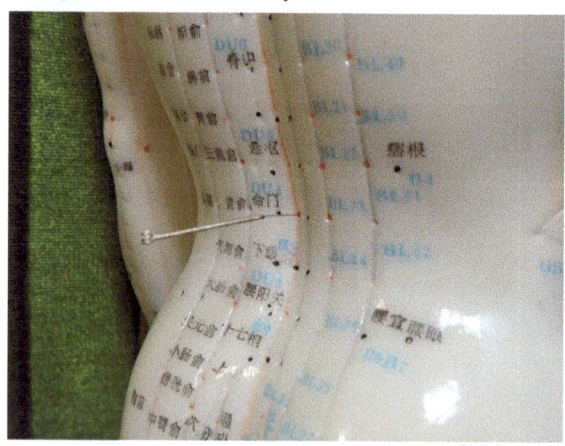

## Energy intake and delivery points

Yongchuan. When we "claw the toes" a hollow is created below the base toe joints. Point kidney 1.

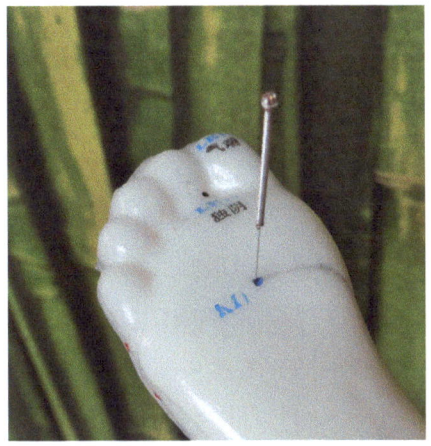

Laogong. If we tip the tip of the ring finger into the palm of our hand, we come to this point.

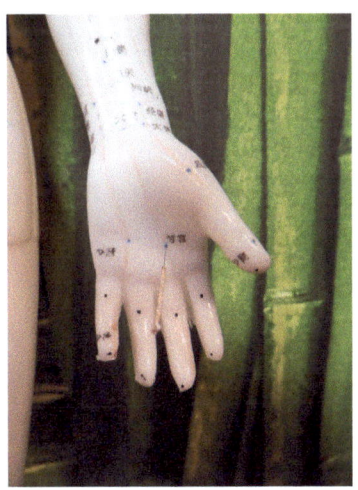

## About this series of exercises

This series of exercises has its origins in the Song Dynasty (960-1279). These exercises were developed around the Tai Hu Lake and later modified. The Tai Hu (Pinyin Tài Hú - "very large lake") with 2250km² is the third largest freshwater lake in China. It is located in the Yangtze River Delta in the south of Jiangsu Province near the city of Wuxi.

The energy intake is stimulated, the muscles strengthened, the mobility improved, the blood flow to the internal organs and the oxygen uptake are increased. The imitation of animal movements and the movements of a lake resident stimulate the imagination of children and also make adults happy. You don't need to complete the entire exercise series, you can also take out individual exercises for your daily exercise program.

## Basic position

Stand feet shoulder-width apart and parallel.
Bend your knees slightly, but not beyond the tips of your feet.
Tilt the pelvis forward and down so that the lumbar spine straightens. For people with a hollow back, this is often difficult at the beginning, the upper body leans back. This should be straightened out.
The spine should be as straight as possible.
The chin is lowered slightly, the cervical spine is stretched.
All nerve impulses can flow more freely.
Take your shoulders back, then let your arms hang loosely. Relax your shoulders. Move your elbows slightly to the side. This creates some space in the armpits.
The hands are not stretched, loose, but slightly stretched in the palms to absorb energy. Slight, involuntary movements of the fingers are a good sign when consuming energy.
We can imagine that the feet, like the roots of a tree, reach deep. The upper body is movable like the branches of a tree without giving up the basic position described above.

Try to calm down, to absorb nature and the life energy in it. In addition, the inner mindset should be like an empty white room. The basic state should be taken for 1-2 minutes before and possibly between the exercises in order to feel the effect. In the basic state we breathe through the nose, during the exercises we breathe in through the nose and out through the open mouth.

Since we at Qi Gong open up exercises for the Qi of the environment, we should not practice in strong wind (creates so-called "wind diseases"), on a raging river (the energy is deprived), before a thunderstorm (puts us under tension) or with fever (increased). In case of coronary artery disease, exercise in consultation with the teacher.

## Preparation

With a loose right fist from the left shoulder to the left elbow, tap to the left hand with loose strokes. Turn the inside of the forearm upwards and tap from the wrist up to the crook of the arm and further to the armpit. Change back to the shoulder there and tap down on the outside. 8 circles. Then change sides and repeat on the right side.

Form both hands into loose fists and pat down on both sides of the legs, from the hips to the ankles. Knock on the inside of the leg from bottom to top. Move towards the hips in the groin area again. 8 circles.

From the basic stand, turn the pelvis and upper body to the right and left. Swing your loose fists and onto the energy center Dantian (approx. 2 finger widths below the

Belly button) and knock on the opposite energy center MingMen. About 1-2 minutes. Then move your fists a little higher and tap the right and left chest and kidney alternately.

## 1) Stretch to the sky

Inhalation: Clasp your hands over your head, stretch your palms up, tiptoe.
Exhale: lower your feet, release your hands, crouch a little, move your arms down so that your elbows rest on your knees.

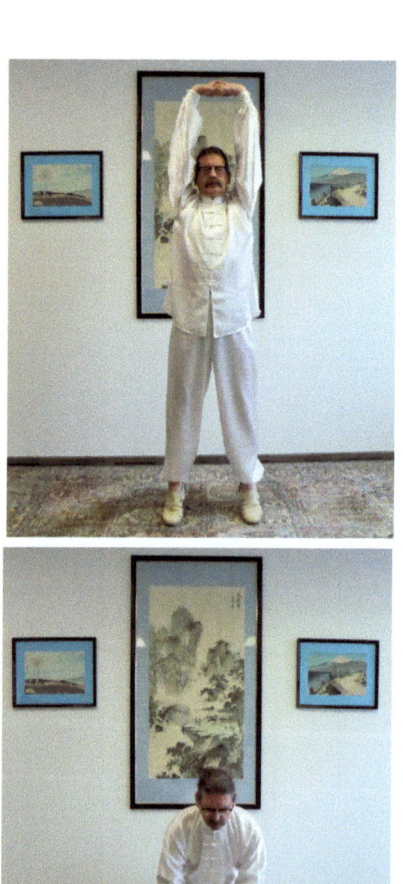

## 2)Lift a leg

Inhalation: Put both hands on your hips and lift one leg to the side, ideally up to the right angle.
Exhale: lower leg
8 x each side

## 3)Bend your knees

Slight tackle, feet slightly outward. Put your hands in your sides.
Exhale: crouch, leave your anus and lower abdomen loose. Back straight. Inhalation: straighten up, tense the anus and lower abdomen. 8x

## 4)Rowing

From the basic position, put one foot forward. Shoulder width, parallel and so that the heel of the front foot is at the same height as the toe tips of the rear foot. The hands hold an imaginary rudder. Inhalation: Pull the rudder towards your body and shift the weight onto your back leg. The back knee is bent, the front knee stretched. The toes of the front foot can lift off slightly.
Exhale: Push the rudder forward and shift the weight onto the front foot. The back knee is stretched, the front one is bent. The heel of the back foot can lift off slightly.
16 x each side

## 5) Barge

Place feet one behind the other. We grasp an imaginary pole. When the left foot is in front, the right hand is over the left hand.
Inhale: Lift the pole forward. Weight forward, lift back heel.
Exhale: We push off with the pole on the right side. Shift the weight back and lift off the front toes.
16 times, then change feet and hands and move the pole to the other side. Repeat the exercise 16 times.

## 6) Hoist sail

Spread your feet more than shoulder width apart.
Inhalation: Stand on tiptoe, grab an imaginary rope above head height, right hand up.
Exhale: crouch and pull the rope down. 16 x.

## 7)Let the ball circle in front of your upper body

Put one hand on your hip, the other hand moves in a circle in front of your upper body.
The hand position is like an open bowl.
We move the hand 16 times clockwise and 16 times counterclockwise. Then change hands.
The upper body follows the hand movement.
Inhalation: upward movement of the hand.
Exhale: downward movement of the hand.

## 8) Swimming turtle

Put your feet together. Slight crouch.
Exhale: Hold both hands, palms down, in front of your chest. Chin to chest.
Inhale: make a floating forward and outward movement with your hands. Chin up. Squeeze your knees, stand on tiptoe.
Exhale: Both hands return to the chest, crouch, chin to the chest.
8 circles from the inside out, 8 circles from the chest outwards and return in the middle.

34

## 9) Jumping turtle

Inhale: Jump up from the standing position and swing your hands forward and up. Point your palms forward.
Exhale: Back to your feet, let your knees loose and swing your arms back and forth three times during exhalation.
Jump 8 times.

## 10)  Creeping dragon

Stand a little more than shoulder-width apart. Hold hands like dragon claws.
Inhalation: Raise right hand and left knee.
Exhale: Lower right hand and left knee.
Inhalation: Raise left hand and right knee.
Exhale: Lower left hand and right knee.
Alternating right and left. At least 8 X each side.
Like a dragon moving on the floor.

## 11)Penguin

Raise both elbows above shoulder height. Bend your forearms. Hand outside facing the face.
Inhalation: Raise right elbow and right heel.
Exhale: Lower right elbow to shoulder height, lower heel.
Right and left side alternately. 8 X each side.

## 12)Push the ball

From the basic position put your left foot forward. Shoulder width, parallel and so that the heel of the front foot is at the same height as the toe tips of the rear foot.

Hold an imaginary ball on the right side of your body, right hand below.

Inhalation: Shift weight back, back knee loose, front stretched. Hold the ball to the side.

Exhale: Push the ball straight forward. Shift weight forward. Front knee loose, back stretched.

16 times, then change sides, i.e. put your right foot forward and push the ball on the left side (left hand down).

Repeat the whole exercise (2 x 16). Then hold an imaginary ball in front of your abdomen and concentrate on the space between your hands.

## 13) Cardiac massage

Stand more than shoulder width.
Inhalation: Hold both hands at chest level.
Exhale: press both hands forward, down, gently
kneeling.
16 x

## 14) Hand to foot

Slight tackle.
Inhalation: Let your hands hang loosely on both sides.
Exhale: Right fingertips to the left foot and left hand back and up.
Inhalation: Let your hands hang loosely on both sides.
Exhale: Move left fingertips to the right foot and right hand backwards and up.
8 x each side

## 15)Wild goose in flight

Stand slightly wider than shoulder width. Bend your upper body forward.
Inhale: Raise your arms sideways to the horizontal level. Swaying gently as a wild goose moves its wings in flight.
Exhale: Lower your arms
8 x

## 16)The bear

Hold loose fists in front of your ears. The upper body sway to the left and right and trot with your legs on the spot, like a bear.

Inhale: 2 steps

Exhale: 2 steps

## 17)The angler

Place your left foot in front of your right, holding an imaginary fishing rod.

Inhale: Shift weight back, lift your toes at the front. Let the fishing rod circle over your head. Look up at the fishing rod.

Exhale: Eject the imaginary fish hook forward while shifting the weight onto the front foot.

8 times, then put your right foot forward and repeat the exercise 8 times.

## 18) Throw the ball up

Inhalation: Hold both hands under the chest like a bowl. Run your hands up as if you were holding a ball. Guide the imaginary ball back up. The eyes follow the ball.
Exhale: Throw the imaginary ball forward.
16 x.

## 19)   Eject the fishing net

Put your left foot on the ground. Shoulder width, parallel and so that the heel of the front foot is at the same height as the toe tips of the rear foot.
Inhale: Grasp an imaginary fishing net in the lower right with both hands.
Exhale: Throw the net to the front left.
8 x, then change sides. Put your right foot forward and grasp the net at the bottom left. Also 8 times.

## 20) Obtaining the fishing net

Put your left foot on the ground. Shoulder width, parallel and so that the heel of the front foot is at the same height as the toe tips of the rear foot.

Inhale: Grasp and pull up an imaginary fishing net at the bottom with both hands. Weight forward.

Exhale: weight back. Pull the net back upwards and open your hands.

8 x, then change sides. Put your right foot forward and repeat the exercise 8 times.

49

## More books from the author

### Taiji Qi Gong ISBN:9783752820072

In this book there are 22 Taiji Qi Gong exercises described.
These exercises improve energy intake, strengthen the selfhealing powers and bring about a balance of the vegetative nervous system. They promote concentration and inner peace.
They have a positive effect on the digestive organs, the muscles, the tendons, joints and the spine. The increased oxygen intake strengthens the heart and lungs.

### Qi Gong sitting ISBN: 9783750431409

This book describes 34 Qi Gong exercises performed while sitting. From simple movement exercises to Tuina massage exercises, breathing exercises and concentration exercises.
These exercises improve the energy intake, strengthen the selfhealing powers and balance the autonomic nervous system.
They promote the ability to concentrate and inner peace.
They have a positive effect on the digestive system, the muscles, the tendons, joints and the spine. The increased oxygen intake strengthens the heart and lungs.
It is very well suited as a exercise book for occupational medicine, for old people's home, as a com pletion for any Qi Gong course or just for in between for all office or computer workers. The many photos and the clear description make it easy to understand the exercises.

Qi Gong stand exercises  ISBN9783751907323

In this book 23 Qi Gong stand exercises are described. These exercises improve energy absorption, strengthen the self-healing powers and balance the vegetative nervous system. They promote concentration and inner peace. They strengthen the muscles and tendons. The standing positions of the 5 animals (monkey, deer, bear, tiger, crane) are also suitable for children.

Medical Qi Gong according to Prof. Wu

ISBN 9783751904575

This book shows exercises that include have an excellent effect on the following symptoms: high and low blood pressure, stomach and intestinal complaints, lung problems, insomnia, nervousness, lack of concentration, lack of energy, back pain and excessive stress.
With regular and persistent practice of Qi Gong, practitioners can improve their health and find inner peace and relaxation.
Since the exercises can be carried out with different levels of effort, they are also suitable for older, weakened people.

The books are available in any bookstore or on the Internet at Amazon or at www.bod.de. A small preview is also possible there. Also available as an e-book.